All About Allergies

Contents

What are allergies?	2
Your body's defences	4
Your immune system	6
How do allergies start?	8
Some common allergies	10
How you can help	18
Glossary	20
Index	21
Allergies and triggers	22

Written by Catherine Baker

Collins

What are allergies?

Our bodies are brilliant at fighting off **germs** that could make us ill. But sometimes, people's bodies start to fight off things that aren't germs. These can include some types of food, **pollen** and even animal fur.

When this happens, it can make the person feel unwell, and we say that they have an allergy.

Allergies are very common.

Did you know?

Worldwide, one in three people has at least one allergy!

Your body's defences

Your body is defending itself against threats all the time.

For example, every time you blink, you're getting rid of dust that could make your eyes itchy.

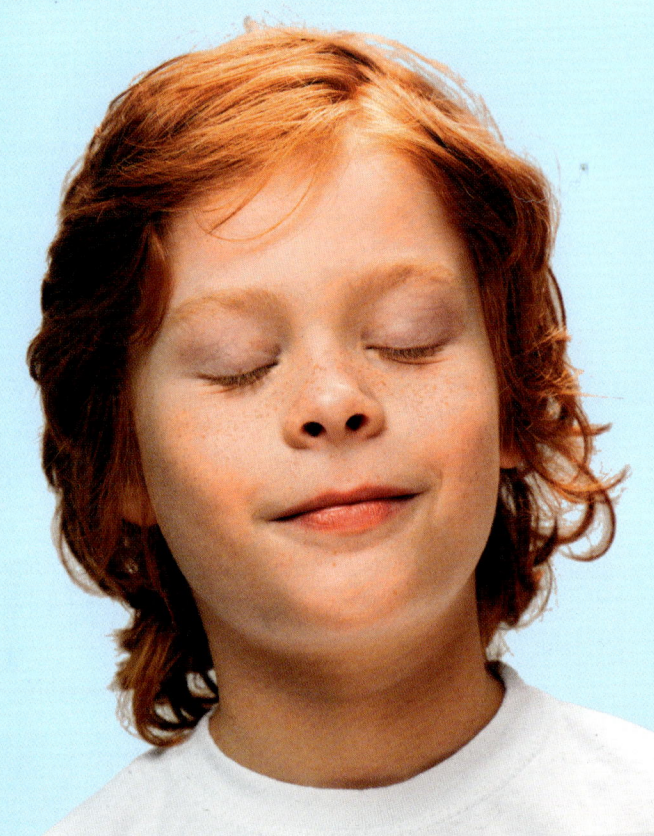

Did you know?

Your nose is also good at keeping bad stuff out.

Even your snot can trap **bacteria** and other harmful things before they reach your lungs.

Your skin protects your insides from danger too.

Sometimes, harmful bacteria and **viruses** do get inside us. But don't worry! Your immune system is there to protect you.

Your immune system

Your immune system is a bit like an army that's on the lookout for enemies. The soldiers in this army are called white blood cells (WBCs).

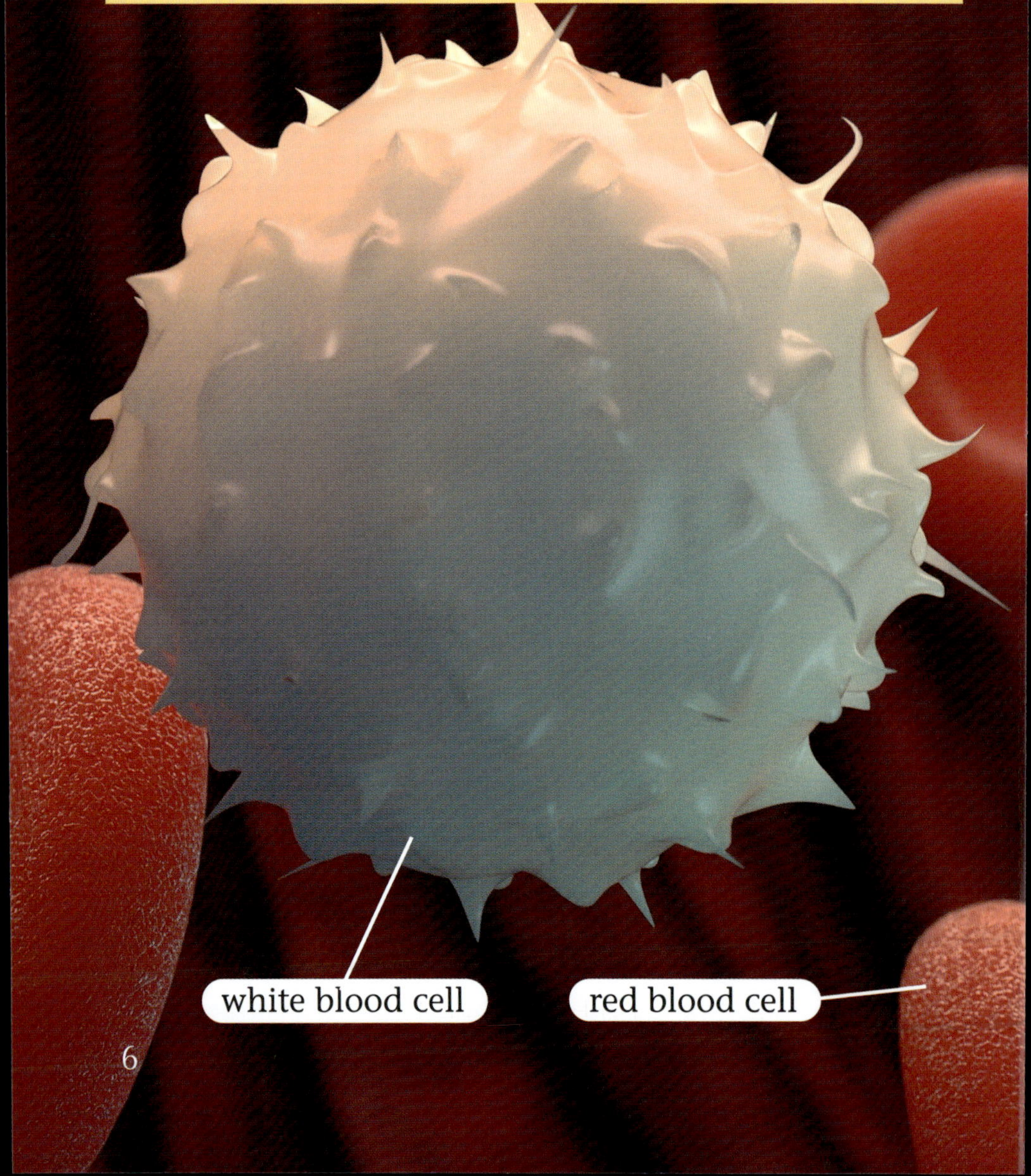

white blood cell

red blood cell

When the WBCs find an infection, they start to produce antibodies. These are like a special weapon to destroy the infection.

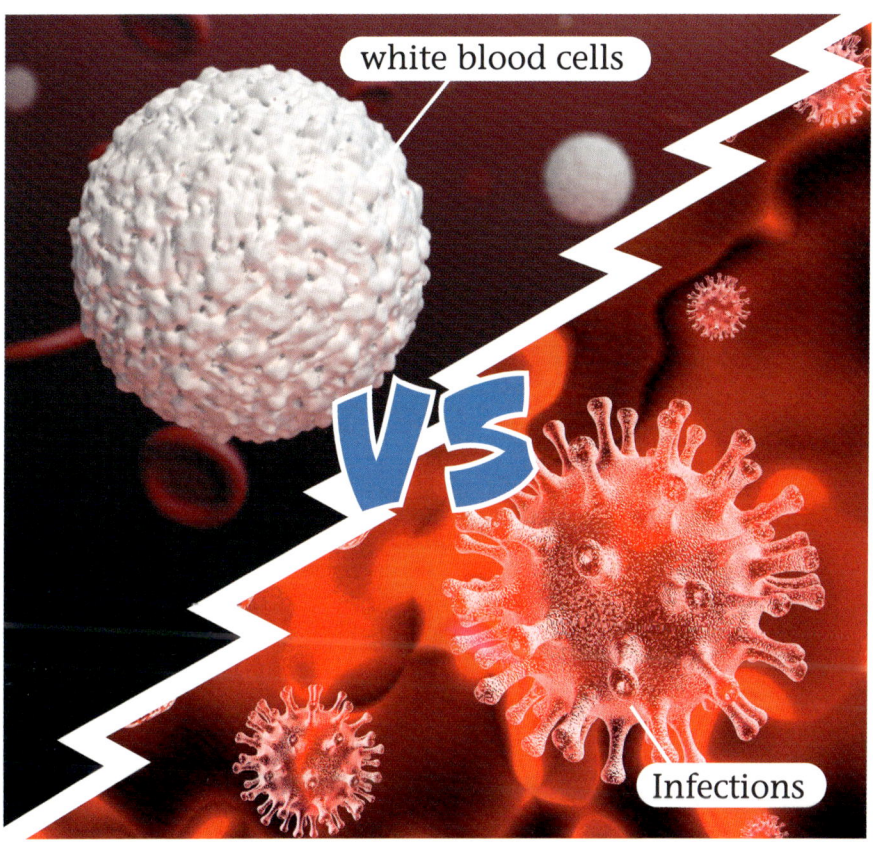

Once your WBCs have made antibodies to fight against an infection, they will do that again and again! Every time you come into contact with that infection, your WBCs will make antibodies to defeat it.

How do allergies start?

Allergies happen when our WBCs make a mistake, and start fighting off things that aren't infections.

For example, someone's WBCs might come across a bit of peanut. Usually, peanuts would not be a problem. But if the WBCs start making antibodies to fight off the peanut, it can cause an allergy.

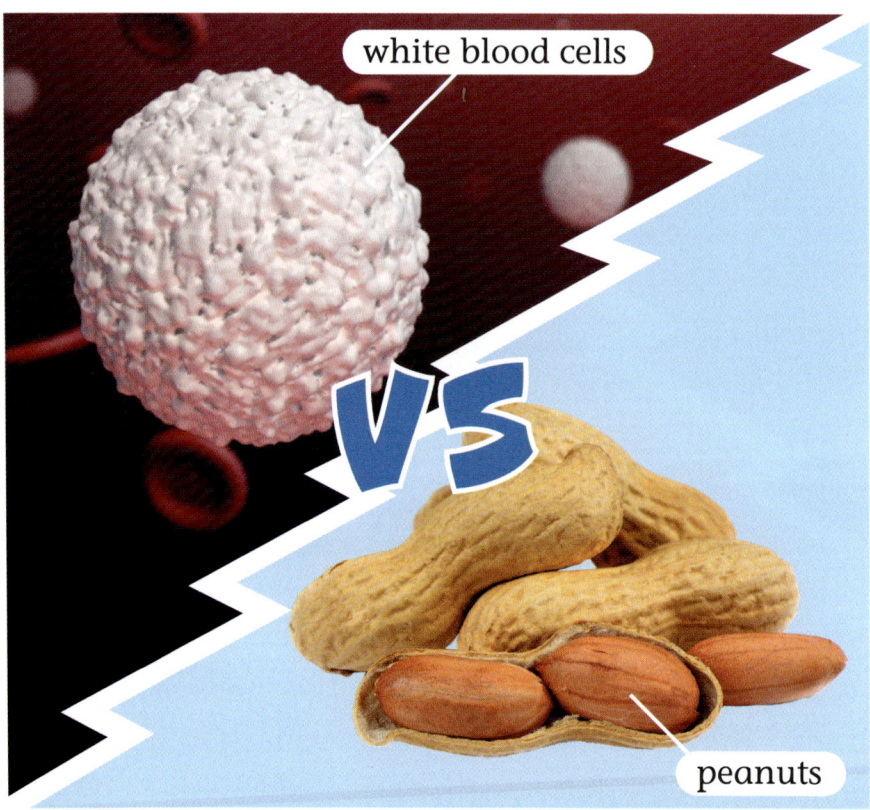

The WBCs produce strong chemicals that give the person an **allergic reaction**, like itching, sneezing and swelling.

Did you know?

Once this has happened once, it usually happens whenever the person comes into contact with peanuts. Other types of allergy work the same way too.

Some common allergies

Hay fever

Hay fever means being allergic to pollen from flowering plants. It's usually most troublesome in spring and summer.

Hay fever can give you a runny nose, itchy eyes and the sneezes! It's not usually dangerous, but it can be unpleasant.

Hamza's story

Hay fever isn't much fun, but luckily lots of things can help. In summer, I take a medicine called antihistamine. It blocks the allergic reaction so I don't sniffle or sneeze so much. I often wear sunglasses as they keep the pollen out of my eyes!

Asthma

If you have asthma, your **airways** sometimes swell and close up, making it hard to breathe. You might cough, wheeze and feel breathless.

Many things can **trigger** an asthma attack – including allergies. People with asthma are often allergic to pollen, animal fur, house **dust mites** or a type of food.

a house dust mite

Lauren's story

I love dancing! Dance is good exercise and keeps me strong, which helps my asthma! If I get an attack, I use an inhaler. It contains medicine to help the wheezing and breathlessness go away.

asthma inhaler

Eczema

If you have eczema, your skin may get very dry, itchy and sore. Lots of things can trigger an eczema flare-up, including soap. People with eczema are often allergic to pollen, house dust mites or **animal dander**, too.

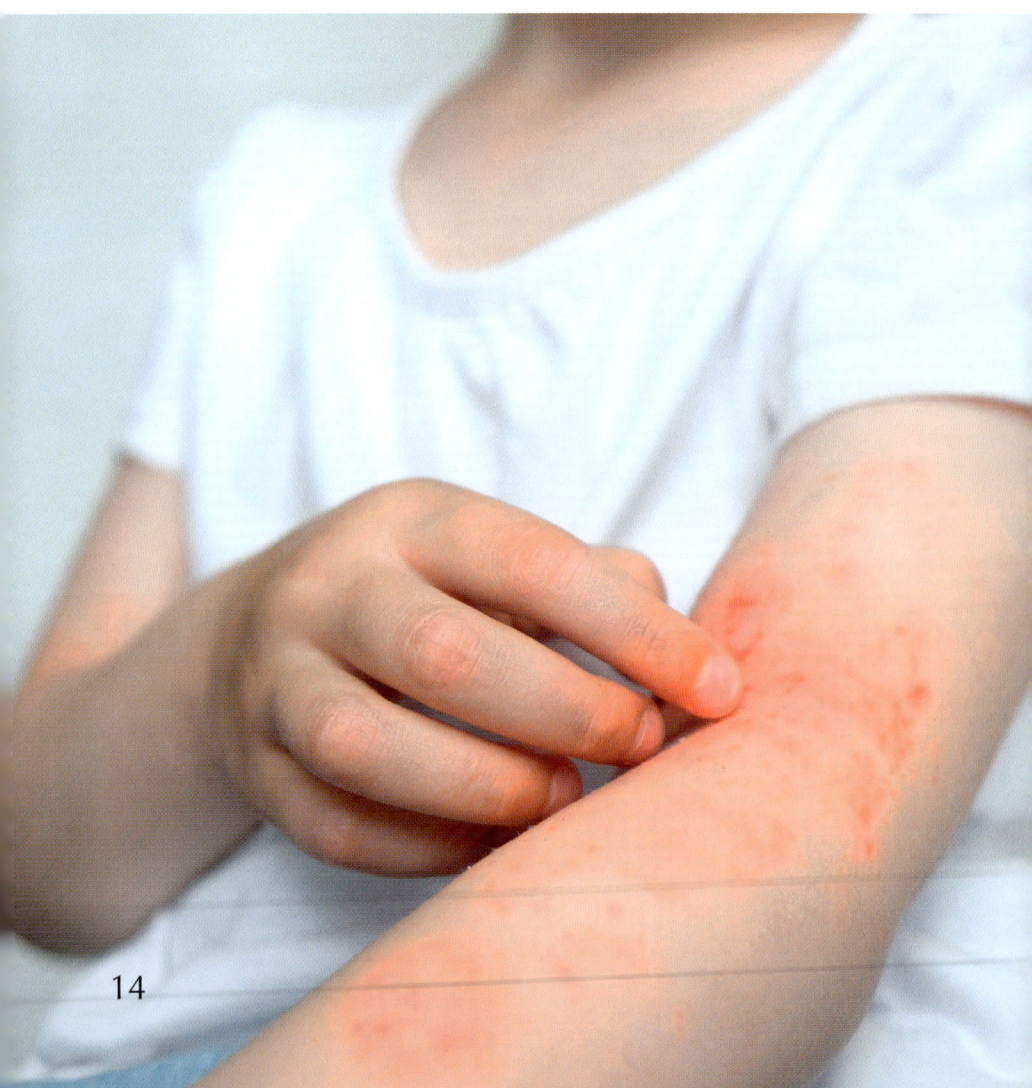

Darcy's story

I've had eczema since I was a baby. It's really annoying sometimes. My skin gets very itchy and flaky. It helps to use moisturising cream – LOTS of it! I wash with special cream too – not ordinary soap.

Food allergies

On average, each classroom will have one or two children that are allergic to a type of food – often eggs, milk or nuts. Food allergies can make people feel very unwell. They might feel itchy or sick, or have problems breathing.

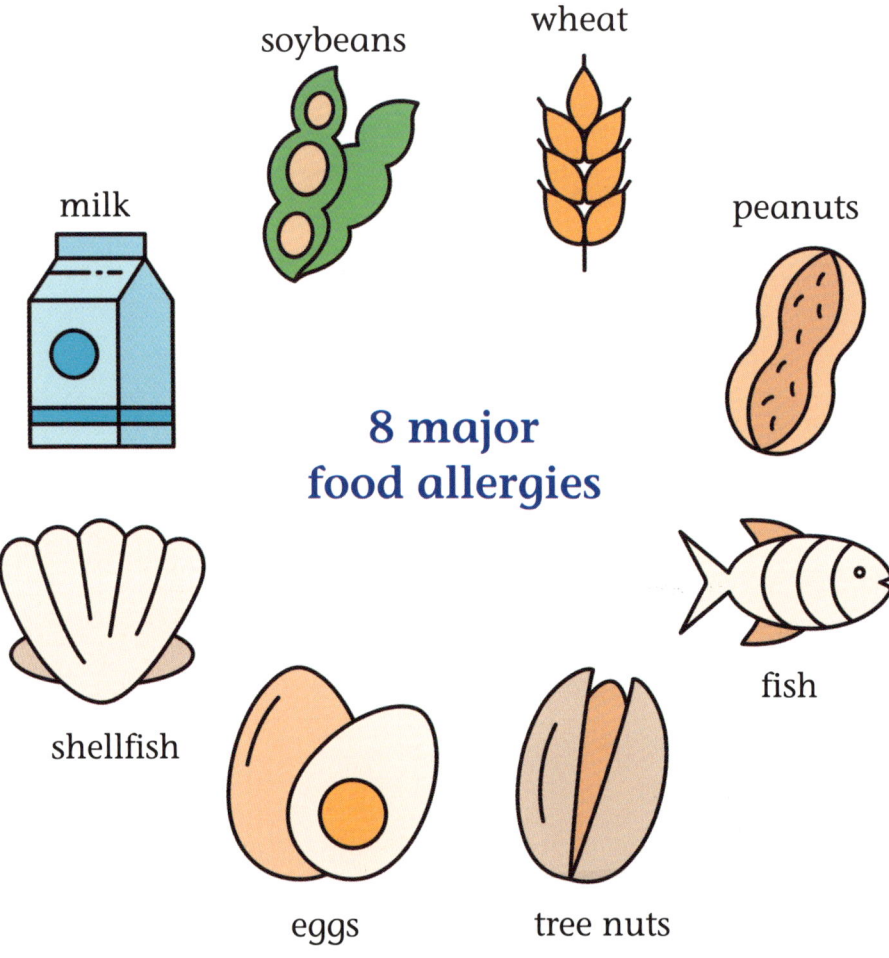

Anton's story

I found out I was allergic to nuts when I was four. I ate a biscuit with nuts in, and had to go to hospital! If I have an allergic reaction, I have to use a special pen to inject myself with medicine. I have to avoid any food with nuts in, which is hard.

injection pen

How you can help

Having an allergy shouldn't stop people from having fun. Here's how you could help a friend with an allergy.

- Find out more about your friend's allergy. Then you can help them avoid whatever triggers it.

- If they have an allergic reaction and need help, tell a trusted grown-up.

- If a friend with a food allergy is coming to your party, ask a grown-up to make sure the party snacks are things they can eat!

Glossary

airways	tubes that take air to your lungs
allergic reaction	when your body responds to something you're allergic to
animal dander	skin cells that fall off animals' bodies
bacteria	tiny things that can live inside our bodies and can be helpful or harmful
house dust mites	tiny, harmless creatures that live in bed clothes and carpets
germs	tiny living things that cause diseases
pollen	powder found in flowers
trigger	to cause something
viruses	types of germs that cause diseases

Index

animal fur 2, 12

antibodies 7, 8

antihistamine 11

food 2, 12, 16–17, 19

hay fever 10–11

house dust mites 12, 14

immune system 5–7

infection 7–8

inhaler 13

injection pen 17

medicine 11, 13, 17

nuts 8–9, 16–17

plants 2, 10

pollen 2, 10–12, 14

soap 14–15

white blood cells 6–9

Allergies and triggers

Ideas for reading

Written by Gill Matthews
Primary Literacy Consultant

Reading objectives:
- draw on what they already know or on background information and vocabulary provided by the teacher
- answer and ask questions
- explain and discuss their understanding of books, poems and other material, both those that they listen to and those that they read for themselves

Spoken language objectives:
- use relevant strategies to build their vocabulary
- articulate and justify answers, arguments and opinions
- use spoken language to develop understanding through speculating, hypothesising, imagining and exploring ideas

Curriculum links: Science: Animals, including humans

Interest words: defending, protects, produce, destroy

Word count: 907

Resources: ICT for research

Build a context for reading

- Ask children to look at the front cover of the book and read the title.
- Discuss what allergies are and any allergies that children are aware of.
- Read the back cover blurb.
- Ask children what they think they will find out from the book.
- Point out that this is an information book. Explore children's knowledge of the typical features of non-fiction. Give them a few minutes to skim the book to find some of the features they identified.

Understand and apply reading strategies

- Ask children to find the contents. Discuss the purpose and organisation of a contents. Ask children to use the contents to find the section called *What are allergies?*